CONFIDENCE NOW!

THE GO-GETTER
WOMAN'S GUIDE TO ACHIEVING
ANYTHING IN LIFE

DR. NEEMA T. MOORE

publish your gift

CONFIDENCE NOW!
Copyright © 2022 Neema T. Moore
All rights reserved.

Published by Publish Your Gift®
An imprint of Purposely Created Publishing Group, LLC

No part of this book may be reproduced, distributed or transmitted in any form by any means, graphic, electronic, or mechanical, including photocopy, recording, taping, or by any information storage or retrieval system, without permission in writing from the publisher, except in the case of reprints in the context of reviews, quotes, or references.

Printed in the United States of America

ISBN: 978-1-64484-574-5 (print)
ISBN: 978-1-64484-575-2 (ebook)

Special discounts are available on bulk quantity purchases by book clubs, associations and special interest groups. For details email: sales@publishyourgift.com or call (888) 949-6228.
For information log on to www.PublishYourGift.com

DEDICATION

I would like to dedicate this book to my amazing twins, Alonzo and Alivia, and my super supportive husband. You have always built me up no matter what challenges I have faced. Your endless love and pep talks have walked me through some of my toughest challenges. When I doubted myself, you were there to give me the push I needed to keep going. I will forever be grateful for all the love, time, and energy that you have invested in me and my dreams. May the words of this book nourish your spirits and give you the confidence you need when you feel that you can't go on.

TABLE OF CONTENTS

Introduction 1
Chapter 1: Mindset Matters 7
Chapter 2: Mental Fitness 15
   How to Choose a Mental Health Professional 17
Chapter 3: Gratitude to Greatness 19
Chapter 4: Wellness Starts Within 23
     Sleep 24
     Water 26
     Nutrition 28
     Exercise 29
         Sharpens Your Memory 31
         Higher Self-Esteem 31
         Better Sleep 32
         More Energy 32
         Cope with Stress 32
         Movement 36
Chapter 5: Honor Thy Self 39
   How to Start a Self-Care Routine 43
     Physical Care 46
     Self-Talk 47
     Spiritual Self-Care 47

- Temporary Self-Care 49
- Long-Term Self-Care 49
- Joy List 49

Chapter 6: Boundaries 51
- Create Your Limits 57
- Tap into Your Feelings 57
- Be Direct 58
- Give Yourself Permission 59
- Honor Yourself 59
- Past, Present, and Future 59
- Self-Care 60
- Speak Up 61
- Start Small 61
- No Announcement Needed 62

Chapter 7: Confidence vs. Self-Esteem 65
- The Importance of Confidence 65
- How to Build Confidence 69
- The Art of Saying No 76
- Confidence vs. Self-Esteem 80

Chapter 8: Put Me in the Game, Coach 85

Chapter 9: Tapping into Your Superhero 99

Chapter 10: Now Go and Be Great 107

About the Author 111

INTRODUCTION

"Adversity is the first path to truth."
—Lord Byron

Life is a journey, and no one said it would be easy. I mean, really, who told us it would be easy? I wrote this book to help people who feel like they have had to face hard-core challenges head-on and who want to find a way to build their confidence to be a better version of themselves and live life full out. This book includes steps that can help you overcome challenges in the darkest of times of your life. When I was at one of the lowest points in my life, I used these tools to help me to create a stronger version of myself. I still use them today. Whenever I am helping people through challenges, I always tell them, I promise you, it will be better on the other side. I created this book to help you get back to your authentic self—and get back to who you were created to be. Ask yourself the question, Who are you really on the inside? And how can you nurture your mind, body, and spirit?

I realized that my true confidence was in jeopardy around 2007 when the world of social media was beginning to open up. I will never forget when I heard through the grapevine that colleges were putting together internet chats to bring everyone together. I thought about how cool it would be if my university had something like that. Then I got the phone call: "Hey, I see they have one for your college!" my friend said. And I was so excited! I thought that this was my chance to really show them that I had made it and that I was not your average ECSU graduate.

So, I remember putting my twins to bed and gathering everything to upload into the system. Headshots included, of course. This was going to be my moment to shine—I mean, most people didn't even have headshots at that point, at least not the average person, so I already felt I was ahead of the game. So, after everyone was asleep, I crept into the computer room and began to set up my very first profile. This would be my opportunity to show everyone who ever doubted me that I had made something out of my life. For some reason, I always felt like an underdog.

At this time in my life, I held two degrees, one in secondary education with three years of teaching in the public school system under my belt. I had earned my doctor of chiropractic from the prestigious Palmer College of Chiropractic and I owned my own practice. My husband and I had bought a beautiful house with a big backyard where the children could play. The neighborhood was an adorable neighborhood, and we lived right in the cul-de-sac, which was my dream come true for a family home. I was a doctor with the sweetest boy/girl twins and married to a tall, dark, and handsome husband that had also become successful and had a great job in education.

Of course, this was the moment I could show all my ex-boyfriends what they had missed out on in life. As I sat there uploading my accomplishments into the abyss of a social media profile, I realized that the reality was that I wasn't happy and what I was posting was just a façade of what my life was really like—which was a miserable, unhappy marriage, and feeling super alone in my life because I had not focused on what brought me joy. My spouse at the time had done a good job highlighting my weak points, so overall, even though I may have looked successful on the outside, I felt pretty miserable about my life on the inside. That is the moment I knew I had to make changes in my life to get back to my authentic self as well as create a new and better version of myself.

After I had the realization that I needed to make different decisions in life, I made drastic changes, like getting a divorce, moving out with my twins, being a single mom for two years while running my practice alone, and I adapted to being a single mom with very little support. It was difficult—I mean very difficult—and there were many days I cried in between patients, trying to figure out what the heck I was doing with my life and where I had gone wrong. During that time, I got back to nurturing my mind, body, and spirit. In this book, I have included the tools I used to get me through, and I hope it helps you too.

As you go through life, life's challenges begin to chip away at your self-esteem and self-confidence. Here is a little of how I got to a place of feeling like I lost some of myself over the years. Over time, life's challenges chipped away at my confidence. I feel so blessed to have had the opportunity to become a wife and a mom. Going through childbirth and carrying my twins forty weeks to full term is a complete blessing, but it definitely takes a toll on your body, and I don't look the same as I did when I was twenty years old. As wonderful as childbirth can be, giving birth can be a confidence snatcher. Opening your own practice and putting so much pressure on yourself to be successful while having young children at home wears you down. You are tired; you sleep when you can. You begin to age. Confidence snatcher. You realize you need to make a real, adult, heartbreaking decision in your personal life and get a divorce. You feel guilty, ashamed, depressed, and alone. Confidence snatcher. Being a single mom, wondering if you will ever find love again or die alone. Confidence snatcher. Not to mention, do I even feel like I still have it? Am I still cute? Will anyone ever see me as beautiful?

Phew! If you are a woman reading this, I am sure you understand feeling like this at times. Life can be tough and can be difficult. As life throws you different curveballs, you begin to smile less and less and become jaded, bitter, and overall less happy—perhaps wondering at times, "How did I even get to this place?" When I found myself at what seemed like the bottom, I was determined to pull myself out of the "sunken place" and reclaim my happiness. I knew it would take work. I knew it was going to take self-reflection, not being a victim, or blaming others for my mistakes and how I got here in life. There has to come a time in your life if you really want change when you take control, stop blaming, and take accountability. Easier said than done, right? But when you are truly ready to change your life for the better and level up, you will do it. As the famous Les Brown says, "When you get tired of lying on a nail, you will get up." With the proper tools, support, and hard work, anything is possible!

No matter what improvements in life we are trying to make, there are steps we have to take first, and that first step will always revolve around our mindset. Getting into the right mindset can allow you to change any aspect of your life. In the first chapter, we will explore the importance of mindset and why it is important for you to begin with this step first as you approach any goals that you set for yourself.

In the chiropractic world, we believe the body works from above, down, and inside out. This means everything that actually comes to fruition in your life begins with a thought first. Your mindset is the one thing that can make or break any goals or direction you set for life. This book is composed of tools I have used to combat the challenges of life on those rainy days of not feeling good enough. These tools will help you keep focused on what is important and teach you to keep "you" as a priority.

CHAPTER 1
MINDSET MATTERS

"Do what you can, with what you have, where you are."
—Teddy Roosevelt

Our thoughts influence our reality. As I said earlier, I was really at a point where I felt ashamed, and quite honestly, like a complete failure in life. When I began to change my perspective on how I thought about my life as a journey, that's when everything truly shifted for me. Instead of thinking that everyone else's lives were perfect except mine, I began to shift to the mindset that we are all on a journey and that my journey is everyone's journey. I began to see and experience joy. While going through my divorce I had asked myself many questions like, "Why me? Why does it have to be me? Why does everyone else get to have a marriage that works out? Why couldn't I figure it out?" The more I asked those types of questions, the more I began to feel like a victim of my own life. No matter how hard I tried I kept thinking, I am a good person; why does this have to happen to me? If I wanted to elevate my mindset, I would need to let those questions go and begin to get into a more positive space.

I began to shift my mindset, and I understood that it's okay to make mistakes. It is more about getting up after falling and facing your challenges head-on. When I began to understand that it was more about persevering than the actual fall is when I began to see life in a whole new light. I began to believe that I could create the life that I truly wanted.

I believe that mindset is where it all begins. The way that you look at the world determines your perspective and your reality. I think the greatest example of this is seen in siblings. You can have siblings that are raised by the exact same parents and be close in age and have different experiences. Both children look at their parents in different ways and how they grew up as well. The reason this happens is that everyone's journey and perspectives are different.

The brain is created to constantly look for danger—emotional danger and physical danger. This is the primitive brain protecting you from the dangers of the outside. We need that part of our brain to tell us not to cross the street, or those red flags that we feel on the inside when we decide not to go someplace or get involved with a certain person. The problem is that our brain is overprotective, and it wants to keep us in the most stable state at all times; because of this, we learn to not take chances that we should sometimes take. We don't take those chances because our brain is telling us that we might get hurt or disappointed or that we may fail in a momentous way. There are so many things that our mind tells us to protect us, but we have to begin to take control over those thoughts and understand that everything that our brain says isn't the absolute truth.

I worked with this lady one time when I was a chiropractor, and she had a daughter who had challenges in school and mental health challenges. She said to me, "I told my daughter, 'You can't believe everything your brain says. Your brain will tell you anything.'" I remember her saying this, and at the time I thought it was the strangest statement. What do you mean you can't believe what your brain tells you? I'd always believed what my brain told me. That is a huge mistake! You cannot believe everything that your brain tells you because your brain is trained to scan for negative things. Scanning dangers all day long prevents us from taking some of the biggest leaps that could change our lives. Our brain's job is to keep us in homeostasis, meaning stable at all times. The problem with that is that there is no growth if you are the same person every single year. You need to try to do things to help your personal self-growth. Personal growth comes out of conquering your fears and pushing through pain. On the other side of fear and pain is the sweet spot. It's where you finally feel that all of your hard work, determination, sadness, blood, sweat, and tears are finally validated, and when that happens no one can take that power from you. This book is about gaining your power back, which is even bigger than just being confident. Many times, we hear the words, "Fake it 'til you make it." It's not a totally bad idea. The idea of faking it until you make it comes from acting a certain way until it becomes a reality. We want to get past the "faking it" and for you to truly be your authentic self.

If you are a Negative Nancy, fear not! We are going to talk about some ways to change that mindset. If you want to have quantum leaps in life, you are going to have to take some risks. What everyone has to understand is that there's nothing guaranteed in life. Your mindset will determine how far you will go in business, your life, and your relationships. Your mindset will even affect your health. What we believe happens to us many times. I believe we attract it with our thought patterns, what we believe about ourselves, and what we tell ourselves.

In this chapter, we're going to explore the importance of mindset and how to nurture a positive mindset so that you become more conscious about how you think about the world. We're not talking about denying the reality of the troubles in your life or your world, but we are saying that your perspective and how you look at the world matter. If you can teach your brain to go from negative to positive and realize that no matter what, everything works for your good, you can make magic happen.

As you read this book, I want you to please have an open mind to the ideas that follow. Some of the things that I express in this book you may have heard before; some things may be brand-new, or maybe you may not have looked at them in that way. Controlling how you think and quieting your negative thought patterns can really change your life and your perspective. This can lead to a perspective change in any situation.

Believing in yourself is the first step. If you don't believe in yourself, please don't expect people to believe in your dreams more than you do. You must practice believing in yourself again—what is deep down in your heart can come true. People who have a healthy mindset have faith in themselves and believe that one day they will achieve their goals. They do not let the negative chatter control their outcomes. They also know they are deserving of love, health, happiness, and success.

Setting intentions is a great way to get your mindset in the right direction. What do you want? No, really? What is it that you really, *really* want out of your life? The Oxford Lexico Dictionary says that intention means an aim or a plan. Are you trying to figure out a way to be a more confident you and a more inspired you? This is truly where our first action takes place—it is setting intentions. Setting an intention is about being focused on what you want the outcome to be—determining what you want the outcome to be in any direction in your life. Take some time to get very specific on what you want your outcome to be in your next life goal, personal or professional. Then write it down and look at it every day and every night and every morning. You can do this for every aspect of your life: a date, a meeting, a party, an uncomfortable phone call. A changed mindset works for *all* of it.

Okay, now it's time to get real. I mean, you really have to be honest with yourself and set realistic expectations as you build yourself up. I am not saying to downplay your dreams but be honest with yourself and set realistic goals and expectations for yourself. This means having regular check-ins with yourself to make sure you are being honest with yourself. This also means taking responsibility for what part you play in your life. This is not the time to play the victim and blame everyone else for your problems. You must know that every decision that you have made up to this point has led you here, good and bad. Now, don't go beating yourself up; there is no time for that, we are building a new life, girl! It's time to get real and know you are the conductor, creator, captain, and boss of your own life! You can steer this in the right direction with just a few tweaks in navigation. Just know that playing the victim and feeling sorry for yourself is not going to get you far, and it's time to accept your leading role. Addressing problems head-on and finding healthy solutions are great ways to have personal growth. Complaining and whining about why things couldn't be different will leave you nowhere. When challenges arise, that is the time to face them and figure out a way to overcome them. That is true growth.

Practicing self-love is a great way to change your mindset and learn to love yourself. Self-love is what most people have to work on consistently. You better buckle up, because there is no end destination for this one, as it is an ongoing journey. It's about loving the child within, and what makes them feel loved and safe. Manicures and pedicures and getting your hair done at the salon are not the only ways to show yourself love. It's deeper than that. It is what makes you feel loved, and this will be different for everyone.

How many ways can you show yourself love? Most of us have never been taught how to love ourselves. Take some time to uncover who you really are, what you like, and what you don't like.

One of the ways to do this is by practicing replacing negative self-talk. Let me tell you how to get started on replacing the negative self-talk:

1. Speak to yourself like you are someone you really love and care about. The same words you would use to encourage, love, inspire, and motivate them are the same words that you can use to speak to yourself.

2. Make a list of all the things that you enjoy. And place one a week on your calendar.

3. Sometimes the way to love yourself is just to rest and sleep. Rejuvenate yourself. Don't hesitate to put a nap on your calendar as well.

Be open to learning new things during this process. Mindsets are not as easy to change as we would like to think. You are going up against years of programming, triggers, and past trauma. Stay open-minded as you read this book and as you go along your journey of becoming a better version of yourself. Opening your mind up to new things will allow you to see opportunities where you did not see them before.

CHAPTER 2
MENTAL FITNESS

"The cheerful mind perseveres, and the strong mind hews its way through a thousand difficulties."
—Swami Vivekananda

"Everybody needs therapy." This is one of the first things that one of my coaches said to a group of professional women as we sat there deciding how to build our empires and monetize our degrees. So many of us looked around in awe that the coach would be so bold and brazen to say that we all needed mental health help. I understood what he meant; mental wellness is vital to success. Being a chiropractor, I've seen so many patients come in that have had a lot of physical pain, and a lot of it was due to emotional pain as well. I remember when I had a patient who came in and she had so much lower back pain that her back was really hurting. It was so unusual. I had just seen her two or three days before and she was fine, so I asked her if she was upset about something. She answered back, "I just had a huge argument with my daughter before I came in." People often don't realize that there is a very large correlation between lower back pain and mental and physical stress.

This is when I really began to tie the links between physical health and mental health together. As I would look at my patients who would come in and lie down on the table, I could tell the ones who were happy and had fulfilling lives. I could also tell the ones who were not happy with their lives, who were in my office in pain much of the time. The patients who had happy lives didn't have as many complaints about their physical health. But my patients who were overly stressed, depressed, anxious, or suffering with some type of mental health symptoms had more physical pain and illness.

I believe that mental health is so important and that everything starts with your mind, which we spoke about in the last chapter. This chapter is more about how to stay mentally well. How to be mentally healthy is a subject matter that I feel is skirted over. I didn't want to leave the importance of mental health and wellness out. True mental wellness is more than just positive thinking. Being in the Health and Wellness field, I very much understand that mental health issues are real struggles. As you read this book, if you are suffering from major depression or anxiety, it's important to know these issues are real and that seeking out a professional is imperative to your personal and professional growth. Do not suffer in silence. The tools that I'm mentioning here are just that; they are tools. They are not a treatment for a mental health issue. I want to encourage you to seek out a therapist to help heal your past traumas and to help heal things that have happened to you that you feel like you cannot get over. It doesn't mean that you are weak or that you are an insane person; it means that you are smart enough to reach out for professional help. Mental healing is also part of your success and building your confidence.

HOW TO CHOOSE A MENTAL HEALTH PROFESSIONAL

Please understand all mental health professionals are not created equal. You have to find the one that is best for you, the one who aligns with your values and morals. Someone who truly makes you feel understood and understands what help you actually need.

Your therapist should be encouraging you to make your own decisions and not forcing you or controlling you to make a decision that they think is best for them. This is your life, and ultimately the decisions that you make should be left up to you. Your mental health provider should help guide you and help you to see things from a different perspective, but they should never ever tell you what to do. When you leave, you should feel somewhat relieved, but sometimes you will feel a little bit strained or tired—however, you should never feel bad about yourself or guilty or feel shamed or judged when you leave your therapist's office. If you do experience this, you have found the wrong one. Life is a journey, and sometimes you need a therapist to help you deal with life's challenges.

Anyone suffering with depression and anxiety that lasts longer than two or three weeks should seek professional mental health help. Mental health is important and vital to having confidence. If you are suffering from anxiety and depression, seek out mental health help. One of my favorite resources is psychologytoday.com; this is a resource that I have used for many years, and I refer my clients, patients, friends, and family to this website when they are looking for a psychologist or a psychiatrist.

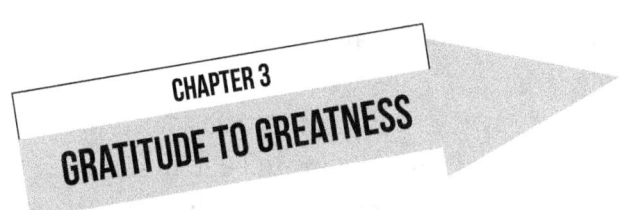

CHAPTER 3
GRATITUDE TO GREATNESS

"As we express our gratitude, we must never forget that the highest appreciation is not to utter words, but to live by them."

—John F. Kennedy

Be thankful that you are here. This is a great place to begin with gratitude. Gratefulness is something that is a true game changer when you are trying to build your confidence or even going through something stressful in life. Listen, every decision you have made has gotten you to this point in your life. Be thankful for all of it, even though you may be thinking, "Why me?" Everything has a purpose, and even though you can't see why, it all works for the good of you. Gratitude is the simple act of saying I am grateful for everything.

Even though you may have had some terrible things happen to you in life, all of it serves a purpose to make you stronger and has made you who you are today. It also allows you to help other people who are going through the same thing as you. Gratitude leads to greatness because it allows you to see the best in everything around you in spite of what it looks like. Gratitude can help you see the positivity in your life.

Gratitude is the secret sauce that allows you to walk with positivity in your heart instead of bitterness. Gratitude is one of those things that can actually help change your mindset so that you can begin to see the world around you in a different way. Opportunities seem endless instead of fleeting. Gratitude also changes your mindset and retrains your brain's patterns. It retrains the primitive part of the brain that constantly looks for negativity.

I want to show you a simple method that has worked for me and that I teach very often to different groups of people when I am speaking. This came from the book *The Happiness Advantage* by Shawn Achor. Achor's research team decided to do an experiment with homeless people to see if they could get them to feel happier about their lives. They weren't actually sure they would be able to make a difference. What they found is that if you practice gratitude in the correct way, you can have incredible changes in your perspective of your life.

We all have learned to say, "Thank you," but I want to show you some new ways to practice gratitude. In Achor's study on gratitude, the researchers created a practice method that allows your brain to scan the environment for the positivity that surrounds you and not the negative. You have to retrain how your brain processes your life experiences. Many times, it is about perspective. Your brain will always want to keep you at a comfort level, but that's not always going to get you to the next level or the life of your dreams.

Here is a way to practice gratitude that will change your life forever. Purchase a journal with a cover that you really like. It could have something motivational on the outside, not just be a regular notebook. I want you to purchase something that feels really good for you to write in. Next, purchase colored pens that you really enjoy writing with. You don't want to write with just any kind of pen. I want you to grab a pen that really makes you feel good. So, pay the extra for a good one. You are going to do the steps I list below for the next sixty-six days to get you in the habit. It has been researched that it takes your brain sixty-six days to form a new habit.[1]

Here are three suggestions for writing in your gratitude journal:

1. Write three new things that have happened in the last twenty-four hours.

2. The simpler, the better.

3. Each day that you journal, it must be something new.

---

[1] Scott Frothingham, "How Long Does It Actually Take to Form a New Habit?," Healthline (Healthline Media, October 24, 2019), https://www.healthline.com/health/how-long-does-it-take-to-form-a-habit.

When researchers did the study with the homeless people, they found that when people didn't think of three different new things every day, there was no change in how their brain viewed their environment. Change in how you see the world begins when you can see the blessing that is already occurring in your everyday life. Every single day, you should be writing something in your journal, preferably in the morning or the evening before you go to bed—but at least once a day. This will help to change your mindset as well as make you feel better about what is going on currently in your life. No matter what is going on in your life, there's always something to be grateful for. The more you can appreciate the simple things in your life, the more you can see the joy that already exists right before your eyes.

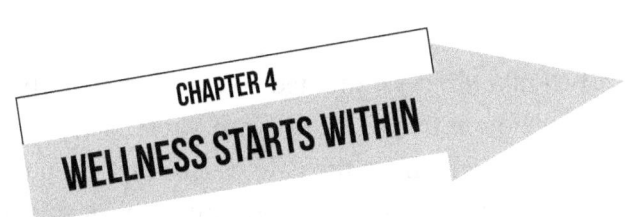

CHAPTER 4
WELLNESS STARTS WITHIN

"The doctor of the future will give no medicine but will interest his patients in the care of the human frame, in diet, and in the cause and prevention of disease."

—Thomas Edison

Health is your superpower. It is ultimately the one thing that if we don't have, our hopes and dreams can come tumbling down like a tower of cards. Begin putting your health first and make it a priority. In this chapter, I am going to give you some guidelines on where to begin and what to focus on first. I want you to remember, health will equal your wealth in the long run. The longer you can be here on earth, the longer you have to make your dreams come true. When you are building your confidence, you want to have a solid foundation that you can stand on. Pushing past difficult times is going to take all of your strength, health, and energy. It is important that you understand that being healthy is a huge part of feeling confident. In this portion of the book, I am going to list some tips that can help you get started on your health journey. So, let's get started.

SLEEP

Many of us take sleep for granted. We don't realize the importance of how it helps us deal with stress. Sleep is your body's recovery time from the day; it also allows you to put your brain to rest. This is so important when it comes to making decisions about the hard things in life. Despite what people have told you about sleep, like "You can sleep when you're dead," you need sleep. At least eight hours, to be exact. Yes, as an adult you still need eight hours of sleep to allow your body to heal and recover from the day. If you don't get the sleep your body needs it *will* find it, even if you are in the middle of doing something important like driving or taking care of your children.

Sleep is involuntary. That is why we hear of people falling asleep on the road so many times. Your conscious mind does not control your sleep.

Sleep is important for you to potentially avoid burnout. Aim to get eight hours of sleep and try to go to sleep before 10:00 p.m. every night, especially if you plan to wake up around 6:00 a.m. When you get proper sleep, you are most likely to reap the benefits of relaxation and energy balance. The most beneficial part of sleep is restoring your body and brain from the stress of the day.

Studies show that four to five hours of sleep can lead to negative impacts on your life, such as becoming sad and angry quickly. Lack of sleep makes you overall more emotional. The lack of sleep can cause you to behave in a way that you normally wouldn't, which can cause you to have problems in your relationships, as well as make bad business decisions and give off negative energy. No one wants to be around a negative person, and they definitely don't want to do business with them.

What I suggest for everyone is building a sleep routine. A sleep routine can help you to decrease your distractions and increase the time that you are sleeping.

Sleep is so important that it actually can help you avoid emotional burnout and give you immunity. Building a sleep routine creates boundaries and decreases disturbances, which allows your body to actually welcome sleep.

Here are some tips for creating your sleep routine that I practice:

1. Turn off your electronics thirty minutes before bed. This includes your cell phone and laptop.

2. Find a good pillow. You need a good pillow, or you may possibly want to sleep without a pillow at all. A proper pillow can allow you to place your head in the right position for a good night's sleep.

3. Decrease the lighting that is in your bedroom. This will make a huge difference in you getting to sleep and staying asleep. Shutting off the light of your

electronics will allow you room to be prepared for sleep.

4. I really would suggest a sleep mask. A sleep mask that covers your eyes can block out any light and cause your body to go into a full state of sleep and a deep state of REM.

5. Try meditation before sleep. It will allow your brain to reset. Guided meditation can help your mind to calm down for the day.

6. Avoid caffeine before you go to bed. If you want to improve your sleep, you do not want to drink caffeine. Caffeine is your enemy when it comes to sleep. It is very important that if you are drinking a tea, it is a relaxing tea like a chamomile tea or a soft tea that allows you to relax and get your rest.

7. Make sure your bed is comfortable. A bad bed can steal your sleep without you even knowing it. A new bed can do wonders for your sleep patterns.

WATER

Water, Water, Water. Water is the ultimate key to health. You can live several days without food, but you cannot go any days without water. That is because it is so vital to the body in all of the processes it undertakes to keep you alive. So, you can imagine that if you are stressed and dehydrated, this will affect how you show up. If you are going through a stressful time in life, you need more water. Stress is very dehydrating to the body functions that are needed on a daily basis to keep you alive and feeling well without illness.

Water helps with detoxifying your body and keeping the arteries clean. It is recommended that you drink half of your body weight in ounces.[2] It is important to note that if you are working out or drinking caffeine, this can cause your body to dehydrate even faster. Adding fruits and vegetables that have a high water composition can also increase your hydration from the things that you eat, such as cucumber, celery, tomatoes, radishes, cauliflower, strawberries, and broccoli. It's important when you're working out to replenish your sweat by drinking more water. If you are working out, replenish your water while working out. Drink water not only during your exercise routine but before and after as well.

If you are like so many of my patients who don't like to drink water, there are so many different things that you can put in your water to make it taste better. Lemons, mint, oranges, cucumbers, or strawberries can really help spice up your water intake. Even getting a cute water bottle or one with reminders can help as well.

---

[2] Holly Van Hare, "We Asked 10 Nutritionists How Much Water You Should Actually Drink," Jan 6, 2016, www.thedailymeal.com.

NUTRITION

Nutrition can help tremendously when you are trying to build your confidence as well as avoid burnout. You cannot be awesome, amazing, and build your empire if you feel unhealthy. Feeling a lack of self-confidence can increase when you have an unhealthy diet that keeps you feeling down, tired, and depressed. To get back on your game, nutrition is going to be a huge part of how you feel and how your body functions. Diet can impact so much of your physical and mental health. In order to properly heal physically and mentally, you have to give the body what it needs to thrive. Creating a healthier diet and swapping out unhealthy foods for healthier options can make you optimize your health, lift your mood, and make better decisions.

Often, continuing to eat as we did as children has formed bad habits. Yes, what our parents have taught us is not going to serve us as we build confidence. Now that you are an adult, it doesn't mean you can eat whatever you want, especially when you get over thirty. That will catch up with you, believe me. When you are improving your mindset and changing your life for the better, you don't want to feed your body food that does not fuel you.

So, let's get into some ways that you can actually begin to add some easy nutrition adjustments to your life. This is not something that should be overwhelming, and do not try to do everything all at one time. Don't try to exercise, change all of your old eating habits, journal, and meditate all at one time. Long-term change takes time.

Let's begin with some helpful changes that you can start now. Meal prepping is a great way to begin your healthy nutrition journey. Meal prepping helps keep you on a healthy regimen. Begin with creating a list of healthy meals you would like to eat. Get the ingredients and choose a day to actually create your meals. Ideally, you want to create your meals for at least five days during the week. If you are not into meal prepping, I suggest ordering from some of the wonderful companies that prepare and ship healthy meals right to your home. It's easy and allows you to keep going without taking too much time to create meals.

It's important to remember that your diet will affect your mood, your weight, and how you feel on a daily basis. Diet also has long-term effects on your body that may inhibit your health and wellness in the future. Eating unhealthily is definitely a confidence killer.

EXERCISE

Exercise has so many different benefits to it that the list is endless. For almost every condition that is out there that someone is diagnosed with, exercise and a better diet always make their condition better. There are very few diagnoses and health challenges that are worsened with better diet and exercise. Exercise can help with stress, it can help with feeling overwhelmed, and exercise literally changes your body chemistry.

Exercise can help you lose weight and get stronger. And if you want a quick boost of confidence and to feel like you are ready to kick butt, exercise is where it's at! You will start to feel more empowered, confident, and in control of your life. Some of my best ideas for my business have come to me while I was working out. I know many people don't really want to exercise because they feel that it doesn't give them the results quick enough, or they just don't want to do it. Exercise has so many benefits that it really outweighs not exercising at all.

What I like to tell my patients is to start small. Using the word *exercise* makes it seem like a chore and not fun. So, I tell my patients to work on moving their bodies. Get into movement! Move your body around, whether it's stretching, running, yoga, or walking. It doesn't have to be something that is high intensity for it to be beneficial. Low-impact exercising is still very beneficial for your physical and mental health, and it also helps decrease your stress levels. Whenever I begin to exercise, I get a feeling of being able to finally take control of my health and my body. Exercising allows you to be at the helm of your own health. It also reminds us that we are the ones in control of the direction of our lives.

Isn't that the best feeling in the world? Knowing that you actually have control over your life, over your health, over the direction of where you are going in life? Adding another thing to do to your schedule seems like a lot, but it won't take much to really make a difference. I promise you, once you begin to exercise—even if it's for five to ten to fifteen minutes—you will start to feel more empowered about your life in your body. What I tell my clients and patients to do is to start small. Start with just fifteen minutes of an activity that you'd like to do and work yourself up to a full thirty minutes and then a full forty-five.

So, let's talk about the advantages of exercise and the benefits it can have for your body.

Sharpens Your Memory
Exercising sharpens your memory and your thinking. It allows for endorphins to be released that allow you to feel better and actually support and aid in concentration and mental sharpness. Exercise also promotes the creation of new brain cells, which allows for your body to benefit from anti-aging as well.

Higher Self-Esteem
Exercising on a consistent basis boosts your self-esteem and makes you feel that you have more control over your life. And it empowers you; if you make it a habit, you will feel a

sense of accomplishment even if you take very small steps to achieve and work toward your fitness goals.

Better Sleep
Even small amounts of brief exercise that last only ten to fifteen minutes can allow your body to sleep better. The best time to do exercises—early morning or late afternoon—actually help you to sleep better. If you decide to exercise at night, make sure to choose something that is more relaxing such as yoga or stretching to help you sleep better.

More Energy
Exercising allows you to have more energy. It actually doesn't make you feel more tired. However, it *can* if you start off feeling that way. Starting off with small increments can actually boost your energy throughout the day and cause you to feel more alert and awake. You won't feel as tired as your day goes on. It's amazing how actually working your body and using your body can give you energy, and not take away your energy like most people think.

Cope with Stress
Consistent exercise can help you with your mental wellness, help you develop mental toughness, and help you to cope with the daily stresses of life. This is much better than feeling like you need to turn to other supports such as alcohol, tobacco, increased fatty foods, or even bad relationships. Most people use the things previously stated to help them relieve

stress and to help them cope and deal with challenges that come along with daily life. Exercising will help you develop a stronger resilience to deal with your mental stresses better than if you use a negative coping skill. Even a little bit of movement is better than no exercise at all.

I can't express enough that it's so important for you to listen to your body when it comes to exercising, especially when doing things like stretching, cardio, running, cycling, and even walking. If you feel pain while doing these exercises, it is important to stop when you feel pain and not try to push past the pain. Often, people end up injuring themselves even more by not listening to their bodies. If you are someone who has never exercised before or is unsure about adding it to your current health routine, make sure to consult your doctor.

So how can you get started in the easiest and quickest way? Let's create your plan below:

1. Start small when you have not been exercising on a regular basis. It's important for you to start with very small increments of exercise—either the waiting time or the number of reps that you are trying to complete. When starting off with some type of cardio exercise, begin with a small increment of time. I usually even recommend anything from five to fifteen minutes, beginning with that amount of time and then increasing it to one to five minutes

every single day. When dealing with weights, try doing at least one to five reps your first time lifting an uncertain weight. If that feels good, move on to doing more reps with that particular weight. When stretching or holding a certain position during yoga, try holding it for one to five seconds and just increasing it a little bit every day. When you are starting off with any cardio or exercise, it's important for you to remember to also check with your doctor to see if he or she recommends you begin an exercise program.

2. Schedule your workouts at a time where you feel the most energized and when you feel your absolute best, and also think about when it's best to fit in your schedule. I want you to remember that exercise does not have to be a lot of time. Fifteen minutes can do the trick as long as it's done consistently. You don't have to exercise for forty-five minutes to an hour every day to feel the difference, or see the difference, and have your energy boosted throughout your day.

3. Make sure to wear comfortable clothing when you are exercising. I even recommend buying some new outfits for exercising. There is nothing like putting on clothes that actually match to go to the gym or even walk outside. I really found that when I put

on clothes that actually match and look cute, it actually boosts my mood and self-esteem I definitely recommend getting some new workout outfits. No need for an entirely new wardrobe. Just pick up a few things that you really like to get started. I suggest laying out your exercise clothes the night before so that you don't have to spend time searching for them. I mean, lay out everything from your bra to whatever underwear you're going to wear to what you're going to wear on your head, hats and jackets included. Plan it out in advance so when it's time to work out, you are just going to grab and go. It will save you so much time as opposed to allowing it to delay your workout and possibly make you not even exercise.

Now, one of my favorite things to do with exercise is to make sure that you reward yourself. This is something that's really important as you begin to slay your wellness goals. When you think about rewarding yourself, I don't want you just to think about food, of course. Don't reward yourself with sweet treats, and fatty foods that will sabotage all of your hard work.

Try to find things to reward yourself that don't include food, such as a trip, new outfits, a new book, or new shoes. Try to find things that don't involve a calorie count that you can reward yourself with. This way, you're not working backwards on all the hard work that you have put in to burning the calories off.

Rewarding yourself does not have to be for an actual pound loss. You can reward yourself for increasing your reps, increasing your time for cardio, or working out consistently throughout the week. There are many different ways to reward yourself; they don't always have to be you shedding pounds. Remember to celebrate your progress. It's always about progress, not perfection.

Movement
Thinking about exercise can feel overwhelming. Considering getting your body in motion might be easier to grasp.

When you think of movement, you realize you can do that anywhere. Having a dance party can be a great way to get your body moving and actually burn calories. When you begin to include movement into your daily life, invite your friends along with you to make it fun. If you have a family, it's a great time to get your entire family involved, your children and your significant other. Involving your loved ones on your wellness journey will play a big part in your transformation as you begin to rebuild your confidence. Being able to include other people that you care about along in your journey will make it more fun for you, as well as give you that extra support you need to keep going.

Lastly, get creative with your exercise routine. Some of the things I do to get my body moving are short bursts of exercise, like a dance party, jumping jacks, or even walking in place. A great way to get into motion is to create a fifteen-minute playlist of your favorite songs from any era that you like. Put songs on your list that you really like to jam to. Create a jam playlist and dance. Dance like nobody's watching. Partying for fifteen minutes is one of my favorite exercises. It's easy and it allows you to just cut loose and have fun! Mix it up, do jumping jacks, do a variety of movements. It doesn't have to be coordinated or at a gym. Find a space you can move in and go for it! Best of all, this is free, so there's no excuse for why you can't include more movement in your life.

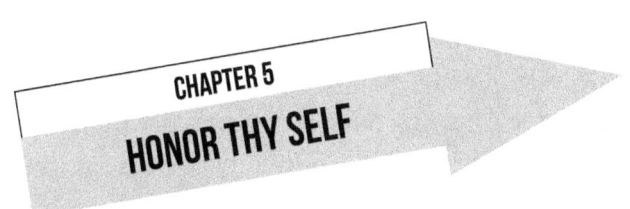

CHAPTER 5
HONOR THY SELF

"Be patient with yourself. Self-growth is tender, it's holy ground. There is no greater investment."

—Stephen Covey

What is self-care? Self-care is the practice of managing and taking care of your own mental health and wellness. There are many misunderstandings about self-care. Many people think self-care is when you are indulging in yourself or being selfish. Self-care entails taking care of yourself mentally, physically, and spiritually so that you are able to keep yourself healthy, as well as taking care of yourself, your family, and your loved ones. This is probably one of the most important chapters of the book because self-care is the area that women seem to leave out the most.

With all the daily activities of taking care of children, spouses, and significant others, we usually leave ourselves last. This causes so many problems for our health and has great effects on our self-esteem and confidence. Putting yourself last can only have negative effects on your subconscious mind.

Self-care is not selfish! Self-care is so that you can not only take care of yourself, but so you can and are able to take care of others. Allowing ourselves to practice more self-care helps us to be able to handle our daily stresses much better. It allows us to be less resentful and less irritable. It allows us to be a happier overall person and a better person to be around.

When we don't take care of ourselves and we think that we're doing our loved ones a favor, it is actually counterintuitive. For some reason, many of us have gotten it in our heads that by being a martyr—putting ourselves last—we are benefiting our family and that being the sacrificial lamb is honorable.

Let's take a look at this in a great example many of us have experienced before, which is getting on a plane. When I used to ride the plane before I had children, I never understood why the stewardess would say to put your own mask on first. I thought, "Wouldn't I want to save my baby first?" As we take a look at this long-standing rule for airplanes, we can see why they tell us to put our mask on first.

There's a reason why on the airplane they tell you to put your mask on first. The airplanes obviously understood the importance of self-care way before it became "a thing." They knew that you can't help anyone else unless you help yourself first. If you don't have oxygen you can't breathe, and then there's no way you can help the people that you love around you, and that is the same thing that goes when it comes to self-care.

Why is self-care so important and critical for your wellbeing? Self-care means different things to different people. Self-care is different for everyone but what is the same for everyone is that it should be done on a regular basis. It should be a practice that you incorporate into your life that allows you to take care of yourself and nurture yourself. Practicing safe self-care allows you to be a happier person, keeps your spirits high, reduces your stress, improves your immune system, increases your productivity, helps with bettering your self-esteem, and of course builds your confidence.

Self-care can even improve your job performance. Self-care also helps with avoiding burnout if you are going through a tough or challenging time in your life. Self-care is a place that everyone can start to help them to heal from their past. When practicing self-care, you really want to ask yourself some major questions like, what really brings you happiness? What brings you joy? Start planning those activities.

What self-care is *not* is only getting manicures, pedicures, going to the salon, getting your lashes done, and getting waxed. All those things are important for your physical maintenance, but that doesn't necessarily mean it's truly getting to the root of self-care, and it doesn't really nourish your spirit and soul. What people sometimes don't consider as self-care goes overlooked.

Self-care is also taking time off from work when you are tired; it's also knowing when you need a mental health day. It's also making sure that you plan some fun into your calendar. Self-care is not going to work no matter what. What I mean by that is, if you continuously think that putting work first and putting yourself last is a form of self-care or a form of pushing forward and being that strong woman, that is not correct. Many people will find themselves very quickly at burnout from not taking care of their mental, physical, and spiritual health. Practicing self-care has actually been shown to increase someone's likeliness to live longer.[3] Did you know that people who exercise and practice self-care are able to reduce their risk of dying?

What counts as self-care? Self-care, of course, should be something that makes you happy. Self-care is not going to be a lunch or a dinner or a holiday or vacation that you must take when you feel obligated to make someone else happy—that is not self-care. Self-care is something that brings you joy, something that you truly enjoy doing, and lastly, something that you can do on a regular basis.

Self-care doesn't have to be something super overindulgent or very expensive. Self-care could be you sitting by a pond, sitting by the ocean, putting your feet in the sand, even taking a nap, or taking a day off. Even saying

---

[3] Moira Lawler et al., "What Is Self-Care and Why Is It Critical for Your Health?," Everyday Health (Everyday Health, Inc., May 19, 2021), https://www.everydayhealth.com/self-care/.

no to something that you didn't want to attend and setting boundaries, which we will talk about in the next chapter. Self-care does not have to be overindulgent, but it can be something that you plan. Making sure that you take care of those things that are important to your daily living, simple tasks such as making your bed, putting lotion on your body after you get out of the shower, lighting a candle that you really enjoy and smells good; these things all nurture your spirit.

For some reason, we have been taught as children that too much of anything is not good—such as too much happiness, too much money, too many joyous occasions; it's just too much goodness for one person to have. I'm here to tell you if you were like me, who was taught that too much fun is not a good thing, you deserve to enjoy yourself every day! Go down your list of things that you enjoy and begin to do them, and it's *okay* if you decide to do one thing you like for self-care once a day. It's *okay* if you decide to do it once a week, it's *okay* if you decide to even do it once a month; the important thing is that you begin to put yourself first. Know that you are valuable and your life matters.

HOW TO START A SELF-CARE ROUTINE

- The first thing that you're going to do is you're going to create a list of all the things that you enjoy doing. I have included a page at the end of this chapter that you can use to guide you through the things that bring you joy. I want you to think of all the things on this list that replenish your happiness, things that you really enjoy doing.

- Pick one of these things that you can do or and put it on your calendar once a week. Some things you may have to plan out two or three days in advance. Some activities you may have to plan out every quarter or every month. The main thing is to get a fun date on your calendar. Just remember, if it is not on your calendar, it won't happen. If it is something you can do on a regular basis, you can make a standing appointment with yourself. I know, if you are like me, you are super busy taking care of the kids, maintaining a relationship, dating, or running a business, which means there's not much time to put on your calendar for fun. That is why it is so important to schedule your self-care. If you are busy like me, you are not going to have time for your self-care, so you must plan it out in advance. There will always be something there that can fill that spot, whether it's the kids, chores, paying bills, visiting a friend, researching something for your business, or taking a class. If you do not plan your self-care, it will not get done. Decide that self-care is important and that putting yourself is an important part of your day. This will boost your self-esteem and help you realize that you can create a life of love and happiness for yourself.

Starting a self-care routine is easy. First you must refer to your "Joy List" of all the things that you enjoy. Keep this list nearby and update it often. I would even put it someplace that you can see every day to remind yourself of the things you enjoy. I have included a list of things that may give you some ideas on how to begin your self-care routine:

- Keep a journal.
- Take five minutes each day and focus on your breath.
- Set goals for each day.
- Make sure you eat breakfast, lunch, and dinner.
- Practice gratitude every day in the a.m. and p.m.
- Put your phone on Do Not Disturb.
- Take up a hobby that makes you feel joy and is not stressful.
- Create a bedtime schedule and routine.

Self-care must be practiced. It's not something that we learned as children, sometimes it can be very difficult to practice, and you may have feelings of guilt. Don't let that deter you from adding this important practice to your life. And I call it a practice because that is what it is: a time and space where you can learn more about yourself. Self-care is how you will heal old wounds and nurture your inner child. When we truly begin to love ourselves is when we create a solid foundation to build on. When you love yourself, that shows up as an authentic confidence in your life that is unshakeable. It's what gives you that extra spark that people can't put their finger on. It allows us to not be shaken when someone says things that are mean or untrue. You can recognize it for what is—not the truth—and move on because from practicing self-care, you love yourself enough to not let the little things get to you. I think the one place in our lives where self-care is needed most is when it comes to relationships. This is when how much you love and value yourself is tested.

When you get into the practice of self-care and self-love, the love for yourself will always outweigh the love someone else has for you, which is ultimately true power and confidence.

Physical Care
There are many forms of self-care. Let's explore some other ways you can practice self-care. Physical self-care is when you prioritize taking care of your body, including anything that deals with exercise, eating healthy, drinking water, and getting enough sleep. We addressed these practices in earlier chapters but in this chapter, doing these things constitutes self-care as well. Anything that's going to nurture your body

and keep it healthy is going to be self-care. Taking care of your mental health is also a form of self-care. Taking breaks when you begin to feel overwhelmed can help with mental stress. Think about scheduling a mental health day. Actually putting a date on the calendar and taking time off from work to take care of yourself can make a difference in your daily performance.

Self-Talk
Analyzing the way that you speak to yourself is a great way to determine where you are in your self-love journey. The kinder you speak to yourself, the more successful you will be at building your self-confidence. How are you speaking to yourself? How do you quiet the negative chatter? Do you speak to yourself as a good friend, or do you talk negatively at every mistake you make? The way you speak to yourself can determine your confidence level. So instead of beating yourself up every time you make a mistake, talk to yourself as a good friend or someone that you absolutely adore and would not under any circumstances want to hurt their feelings. I know that seems extreme, but I need you to use that type of vigilance when you speak to yourself. This type of care is needed when it comes to your self-talk.

Spiritual Self-Care
I know for some of you this might feel a little awkward or tricky depending on how you feel about religion. But don't

worry, this section is not going to be a sermon. I want to talk about spirituality, not religion. This is not about being religious, or even the religion you practice. Going to church or being a good little fill-in-the-blank is not where we are going in this section.

Spirituality is about having a connection with a higher power, a higher power than yourself. It's knowing that there is something out there higher than yourself that is in control that you can actually rely on and go to when you are in your time of need. For me, this is God, but for you, it might be something else. The point I am trying to make is more about a connection to something that is higher than you that you can trust.

Going through this life thinking you are the only one who can guide your life puts a lot of responsibility on you. The responsibility of making the right decisions is based solely on what you know and your experiences. It is obvious that we don't always make the best decisions all of the time. This is why relying on a higher power can take the weight of life off of you and give you comfort. If you don't have this in your life, it is vital that you find this connection and develop that relationship.

Spiritual care would include things like a gratitude journal, meditation, and prayer that you can use to nurture your spiritual health. I would highly recommend you add to your toolbox for your spiritual health.

Temporary Self-Care
Temporary self-care is going to be that lunch with a friend, a massage, or getting your nails done. It's that experience that lasts for a short moment but makes you feel better.

Long-Term Self-Care
Long-term self-care is when you start to develop an actual routine for yourself that you include on a regular basis. These would be the things that you put on your calendar, the standing appointments that we spoke of earlier, or those things that you practice on a regular basis and have become part of your lifestyle and regular routine.

Self-care is something you will have to include in your daily life to thrive and build confidence. Your self-care will always lead to self-love and that is where confidence lives and flourishes. So put these practices in place ASAP! Include self-care not as a once-a-quarter event. This is when you will end up in burnout. Building the blocks for confidence will always start with loving yourself. Start to include *you* on your list of things to do! You will be a happier and more productive person, and you will build your confidence easily.

JOY LIST
What ten things bring you joy?
What did you like to do as a child?

Make a bucket list of places you would like to visit, even local places.
What fifty things have you accomplished and feel proud?
What ten things are you good at?

CHAPTER 6
BOUNDARIES

"You can't control what goes on outside, but you can control what goes on inside."

—Unknown

Setting boundaries is one of those major points of personal development that, when mastered, is a skill that can skyrocket every aspect of your life. It is also the most difficult skill that we will discuss in this book. Most people have trouble with setting, creating, and keeping boundaries consistently. One reason it is difficult is that it usually affects other people. It also usually means a change in how you interact with some of the people closest to you. What boundaries do is allow us to have better relationships with the people who are in our lives, but most importantly, it allows us to have a better relationship with ourselves.

Boundaries end up creating more trust for ourselves. You will hear people say they can't trust other people. In actuality, what they are really saying is that they don't trust themselves. What I mean by that is that they don't trust they can handle what comes next, especially if it is something unpleasant. Setting boundaries is when we draw the line in the sand and understand our values. When we set boundaries, we finally understand that we matter, and we understand that our feelings matter too. Setting boundaries means that we trust ourselves enough to make the right decision for ourselves and put our needs first.

When we don't have boundaries, we begin to do things that are out of alignment with ourselves to make other people feel better. We don't want to be confrontational, or "stir the pot," as they say. We feel that avoiding doing those things is what we need to do to be a good person. We may even end up resenting people who have done wonderful things for us or getting angry when we commit to events or gatherings that we should have said no to. Then we attend the event and stay mad while we are there when we should have said no to attending in the first place. Believe me, that is no way to go through life, just constantly foregoing how you feel to make other people feel happy.

Many of my girlfriends call me when they are considering making a major decision that involves other people's feelings. Often, they just want to make the other person happy, especially when it comes to a romantic relationship. Many times, when they feel like those boundaries are being overstepped and they don't want to say what's really in their heart, I ask them, "Whose feelings matter more?" This is what you need to ask yourself when it comes to boundaries.

Whose feelings matter more? This book is filled with the same undertone, which is to put your own oxygen mask on first. Fill your cup first, take care of yourself, your feelings, your emotions, and your spirit first. Then you will be allowed and able to show up so much stronger and more powerful for the people in your life who matter to you most.

Boundaries are one of the greatest ways to tell what the navigation system inside of you is really saying about yourself. It is a great sign to tell how you truly feel about yourself and how you value yourself and your time. Many times, when we are not setting boundaries, it is due to low self-esteem, low self-love, and low self-worth. One of the greatest ways you can show yourself self-love is by setting boundaries. It sends an indicator to the people around you and to yourself that you matter.

Setting boundaries is something that is going to be a skill that you have to practice and it's going to be challenging. As your life changes, your boundaries will need to change. I want you to think of setting boundaries as something that is ever evolving in your life. This is one of the most important chapters you can read. Creating boundaries around your health, time, money, and self-care is what separates you from living a mediocre life.

As your life and circumstances change, you will need to revisit the boundaries you have set and decide, are your boundaries too rigid? Are some of your boundaries unclear? Is there a situation that has come up for which a boundary needs to be created? Some boundaries will be very easy to set, and some will be really difficult, especially when it comes to your spouse, children, close friends, and even at the workplace. I want you to remember that this is something that will take time and practice. Have patience with yourself and don't beat yourself up. It's not about being perfect, it's about making progress and taking baby steps.

What really prevents us from setting proper boundaries? I have to admit, this is the skill that I have to work on constantly, but I know that if I continue to create boundaries, I will have *more* of what I want in life and *less* of what others think I should have. I have struggled to create boundaries in my life at times due to the usual "suspects": being a people pleaser, wanting people to like me, not wanting to upset people, and avoiding confrontation. For me, boundaries meant that you must tell someone something that they may not like to hear, which means they are going to be upset with you. That never feels good. Like many of you reading this book, I was not shown the proper tools for creating proper boundaries.

What prevents us from setting boundaries? Let's dive into it and see some of the major barriers that usually prevent us from setting boundaries:

1. **Fear.** It can be very scary to try to do something different. What will be the person's reaction? How

will you set the boundary? What will happen if you don't set a boundary? Asking yourself these questions can allow you to decide where this fear is actually coming from and put some solutions or plans in place to actually solve that fear.

2. **Ambivalence.** Ambivalence is having mixed feelings. You may wonder if creating a boundary will make a difference moving forward. The feeling when you aren't 100 percent convinced that setting the boundary will actually solve your problem. It's okay if you don't feel 100 percent sure that something is going to solve your problem, act anyway and take action! Beginning to set a boundary is better than not setting the boundary at all.

3. **You don't know how to set a boundary.** If setting boundaries was not a part of how you were raised, it can be very difficult to try to implement something new. I didn't even know what boundaries were until I became an adult. Thank God for my girlfriend Kate who showed me the book *Boundaries: When to Say Yes, How to Say No to Take Control of Your Life* by Henry Cloud and John Townsend. From this book I realized I had no idea what they were and how to set them.

4. **People-pleasing.** People-pleasing is something that people tend to do more than anything. People like

to be liked. People want to feel accepted, and when you begin to set boundaries—especially if you've been doing things a certain way for a long time—people don't like it when you set new boundaries. This means a change for them, and as my uncle says, "No one likes change but a baby." And even they don't like it all the time. This means that the person who is on the other end of the boundary has to act differently when it comes to you. They may have to change how they respond to you and react to you. People don't like change, especially if they don't have any say in the matter. They want to keep treating you the same because change for them means that they have to make some changes. I want to encourage you to push past feeling the need to people-please. Work toward pleasing yourself and doing what is best for you.

What I stated above are four ways that most people are afraid to set boundaries. I want you to begin to realize that these feelings will show up for you when you are deciding to set new boundaries in your life. This is okay; the point is just to start doing it. Pull your sleeves up and get in the game. Setting boundaries is the ultimate confidence booster. You will begin to feel more valued in your life as well as bring more happiness and joy to your space. I really want you to spend some time creating some new boundaries in your life! If this is something that is new for you, I want you to be patient with yourself and know that it takes time to set new boundaries. No matter if you fail at trying in the beginning, keep trying. The point is to not give up trying but to create your life and live your best life ever.

How do you set boundaries? Let's get into ten ways to actually create and preserve your boundaries. These are some tips that you can use and implement immediately.

CREATE YOUR LIMITS

If you don't know what the limits are, ask yourself where you draw the line? What are those dealbreakers for you in all of your relationships—work relationships, personal relationships, and friendships? Where do you draw the line? Identify your limits when it comes to spiritual, physical, and financial issues. Where do your limits stand? Thinking about what you can tolerate and what you can accept will really help you to acknowledge what makes you feel uncomfortable and what brings stress into your life. Those areas that you feel tension in as you create the limits would be the areas that you have to work on to overcome people overstepping their boundaries when it comes to you. Let's dig in!

TAP INTO YOUR FEELINGS

Tap into your feelings in certain situations. Tap into what makes you feel uncomfortable when you have interactions with people or a particular situation. Begin to ask yourself, what is causing you to feel uncomfortable? What is it about the person's expectation of you that begins to bother you? This is a point where you really have to be aware. Dive deep, get quiet, and become more self-aware so that you can get clear on what it is that really upsets you. Once you have figured out what bothers you, you can begin to figure out how to get on the right path to knowing what it's going to take to set a boundary in this area of your life. Resentment usually happens when someone feels like they're being taken advantage of. Pay attention to those signs. When you feel violated, it's often a sign someone has crossed a boundary.

BE DIRECT

I believe this is the most difficult one to do consistently. Setting clear boundaries doesn't always have to be a direct conversation to actually be accomplished. Setting boundaries will always start with you getting clear and having clarity on what you really want. Being direct doesn't mean that you need to make an announcement to everyone about all of the boundaries you will be making. This is more about creating an agreement with yourself than anyone else. A boundary that has been violated will have to be addressed. When this happens, you may have to have a more direct conversation with who is involved. This may call for a more direct approach, as well as some rehearsal.

GIVE YOURSELF PERMISSION

You must practice setting boundaries. There's definitely going to be fear with how the person is going to react but setting healthy boundaries is a sign of self-respect, self-love, and self-worth. It is okay to feel nervous about setting new boundaries for your life due to the response of people who are used to you behaving in a certain way. In the long run, as you continue to practice you will build your boundary-setting muscles and you will be able to say no and create more boundaries in your life.

HONOR YOURSELF

Honoring yourself means that you are becoming more self-aware, deep-diving into how you actually feel about a subject matter. Ask yourself the questions: How am I feeling? What is the situation making me feel? Is it anger, sadness, resentment, fear? What do I want to change about this situation? What do I want as a solution to the situation?

PAST, PRESENT, AND FUTURE

Thinking about how you were raised can make a big difference in how you handle boundaries. Take into consideration when you're setting new boundaries that this is something that is maybe new for you that you haven't experienced, especially if you come from a family where boundaries were not set or boundaries were often overstepped. It's important to consider this as a learning process and to check-in with all of your relationships to see if you are feeling obligated or overextending yourself in any way. Just remember to tune into yourself and how you are feeling as you are setting new boundaries. We are creating a new future for you, so considering where you came from and what you are creating and planning to do will be something to be aware of as you go along on your boundary-setting journey.

SELF-CARE

We've talked a lot about self-care and the importance of it. Remember that setting boundaries is also a form of self-care. As I stated previously, honoring your feelings is really important when you deal with setting boundaries. It is that awareness of what you are actually feeling and honoring yourself. Creating space for yourself to be yourself. Doing this allows you to be in a positive space. It allows you to have more mental and physical energy. You won't feel as drained because you will have conserved energy by setting boundaries around your time or when someone makes you feel uncomfortable. One of the biggest drainers of energy is saying yes to things to which we should have said no. Remembering that no is a complete sentence can help you tremendously conserve your energy and bandwidth.

Find people who support you in your journey of creating new boundaries. It's going to make all the difference in the world. Trying to do this by yourself can be difficult when you're doing something new you need support.

SPEAK UP

Being more outspoken and more assertive about what is actually bothering you when you are creating your boundary is important. Make sure that you are speaking up for yourself when something does cross that boundary. Get clear on what it is and what you feel uncomfortable about. Like I said before, you don't have to make an announcement that you're starting new boundaries, but when that boundary is crossed with someone, make sure that you are letting them know that that's a boundary that has been crossed. You have to take some time to process how you actually want to say it to that person, but setting that boundary will allow you to gain your power back, feel empowered, and build your self-respect.

START SMALL

As you are beginning your new journey with setting boundaries, start small. You don't have to start with the biggest boundary that you need to set with the most difficult person in your life. Start with something very small. Boundaries can be created around anything. They can be created around your social media time; you can have sleep boundaries or boundaries for how long you are on the phone with a person. I would say make sure when you start creating boundaries for yourself, start with yourself first.

NO ANNOUNCEMENT NEEDED

These are promises that you make to yourself, the most important promises of all. Building boundaries with ourselves is how we work on our trust factor with ourselves that we talked about in other chapters. Start small when beginning to set new boundaries in your life. Once you have started creating some of this muscle, it will get stronger. When you feel you have accomplished one small boundary that strictly deals with you, you can move on to the next boundary that may be a bit more challenging, whether it's something at work, dealing with your family, your children, spouse, or a loved one. Then you can evolve and create tougher boundaries and be willing to stick to them even if others disagree.

Setting boundaries is one of the most important things that you can do for yourself. It is a muscle that you can train. It will take time. I want to impose upon you to be gentle with yourself for this section of your life. Just like when you are in the gym, this muscle will get stronger and stronger over time as you exercise it.

If we think of this skill as a true muscle, we can imagine going to the gym and trying to get stronger. It doesn't feel good as you lift the weights. From a biological perspective, muscles have to tear themselves down to build themselves back up. The body is so amazing in that when we feel pain, it is often our bodies' way of healing and rebuilding to make something even better and stronger than it was originally. Building boundaries for your life is no different from building muscle.

Once you build that boundary muscle, you'll go on to the next boundary that you need to set, and the next boundary and before you know it, you'll be able to set clear boundaries in a way that's assertive, direct, and that honors yourself within that process.

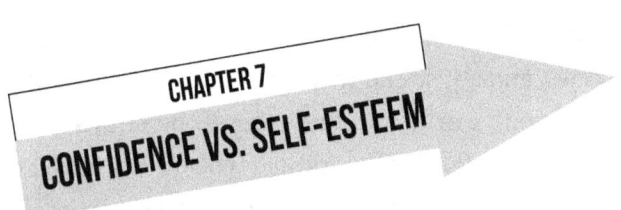

CHAPTER 7
CONFIDENCE VS. SELF-ESTEEM

"Successful people have fear, successful people have doubts, and successful people have worries. They just don't let these feelings stop them."

—T. Harv Eker

THE IMPORTANCE OF CONFIDENCE

I think it's always important to look at a definition of a word and see where the root of it came from. The Lexico definition of confidence states that confidence is "the feeling or belief that one can rely on someone or something; firm trust." Confidence comes from within. I don't necessarily think that everyone is born confident, but I think that life experiences teach us about confidence and allow us to build trust in ourselves.

I think the first stage of confidence in our life comes from being in a safe and stable environment as a child. If you couldn't trust your surroundings as a child, that experience would be the first break in your foundation of building confidence. If you didn't grow up in a safe and stable environment, those experiences could chip away at your self-confidence. Things such as divorce, the death of loved ones, and abuse can make you not trust yourself or the people in your world. When we get to be adults, chipping away at our confidence continues when such situations as closing a business, losing someone important to us, ending a relationship, or a financial hardship.

Building self-confidence can be done. It will take you creating a positive self-talk system so that you are able to build your confidence up when it has been shaken. Building self-confidence is important not just because you want to be able to show off in a crowd, but to show up in your life as a person who can be trusted. If you are a business leader, a teacher, you work for a corporation, or you must present in front of people, it's important for you to have self-confidence. People want to follow a confident person. They want to believe in a person who is confident. Having confidence is important in every aspect of your life! Lacking in confidence can affect every aspect of your life. Self-confidence shows up in every part of your life. When you have it, it's the gift that keeps on giving because people really do like being around self-confident people. It builds trust because they believe that if you trust in yourself, then they can trust in you as well.

To build true authentic confidence, what you must master is the negative thought chatter in your head. As we have spoken about in the previous chapter, resetting and retraining your brain allows you to create a more positive thought feedback loop, which will allow you to see your own power and strength.

There's a reason I started this book with changing your mindset. I knew once we got to this chapter that you would have to open your mind to truly building confidence. When we talk about confidence and learning to change your mindset to a more positive outlook, we begin to see the world in a different way, and it allows us to shift our thought patterns. You begin to ask yourself different questions. Instead of asking yourself more victim-minded questions such as, "Why me?" or blaming other people, it's now about saying to yourself, "Why not me? Why can't I be successful? I can be successful! Why shouldn't I be able to achieve the dreams that I have set for myself?" There is no point in wasting time feeling scared or anxious when you could be out there pursuing your dreams instead.

Asking different questions will get you different answers instead of playing the victim in your life. It's important when you're trying to build confidence to actually begin to feel that you truly do have the power inside of you. Confidence is an inside job. There is no other way around building confidence other than doing the work that you need to on the inside. Confidence is not something that you can necessarily gain from other people; you have to do the work from the inside out.

I asked my son who was sixteen at the time, "How do you think you build confidence?" His response, "My dad told me to fake it 'til I make it." I thought, "This is how it starts." Someone tells us this at a young age, and we take it with us forever. I'm sure whoever said this statement didn't mean fake it 'til you make it forever. I have to hope that they meant fake it while taking action and doing the work but show up and act like you actually have it all together in the meantime. Do the work on yourself while no one is watching until you truly catch up and close the gap to becoming who you want to be.

Faking it 'til you make it can only be done for so long before people actually see the real you. Show up at your best and do the work to become your best self. Faking it until you make it is something that is very temporary and is not going to last long. If you want long-lasting confidence, it's something that you are going to have to work on by healing your past wounds and learning to change that negative feedback loop into a more positive conversation with yourself.

Building self-confidence is not about what you want other people to perceive about you; building self-confidence is about creating self-love inside of yourself and realizing it really doesn't matter what other people think. One of the things that break down a lot of people's self-confidence is worrying about what other people have said about them.

Or what they are going to say about them. You will need to keep in mind that most of the people who are talking about you or saying something negative don't even love themselves, and they don't have confidence in themselves enough to follow their own dreams. Their lack of confidence in themselves puts them on the sideline while you are in the ring of life following your dreams. They are judging from the standpoint that they wish they had the courage to follow their own dreams.

When you think about building your self-confidence, know that you're doing this for yourself, not so that other people. Confidence is for yourself—it is something that you can use in every aspect of your life. Some of the positive benefits of building confidence are greater opportunities, better relationships, a better love life, and even making more money. I believe that confident people do end up having more resources than people who are not confident and play the victim in their life. So, let's talk about some ways to actually build confidence now that we've talked about exactly what it is and why it's so important. This is a section that you will probably want to come back and read more than one time if you are really trying to focus on building confidence.

HOW TO BUILD CONFIDENCE

One of the first steps of building confidence is to look at your past. I'm not talking about the bad parts of your past;

I am talking about times when you showed up and shined bright and showed out! That is the past I want you to think about. Those times in the past when you were at your best and you felt your best, the good times. Just thinking about those moments should raise your vibration. I want you in a place of thinking of your best self.

Now that you are feeling amazing, here is an exercise I would like for you to try. I want you to put down on paper a list of fifty achievements that you are the proudest of. And as you make this list, I want you to pat yourself on the back for what you have achieved that is honorable and good. When you make this list on your postcard or a sheet of paper, I don't want you just to think of the expensive purchase or your achievement you got an award for, but also think of things that you are proud of doing. Maybe it's helping the community, maybe it's being a good parent or volunteering at your church. There are a lot of things that you can be proud of that don't necessarily pay off in a monetary gain. List as many things as possible, and don't mind taking more than one day to ponder over all the amazing things you have accomplished in your lifetime.

Once you have made this list, post it somewhere that you can see it. I want you to use this list whenever you are feeling down and that you are not where you want to be in life. Keep this list close by. When you have those moments that make you feel anxious or doubtful about yourself, this is the place I want you to come to: your Superachiever's List. Reminding yourself of what you have accomplished can catapult you when you are on the edge of something great. When you have something to do that's got you questioning your value or your worth or causing you to ask yourself if "you're enough," this is a great list to use to actually help build your confidence prior to taking on a big task.

Below I will list some activities that you can do to take your authentic confidence to the next level.

- Make a list of all the things that you are really good at: all your talents and all your gifts. Write these on a sheet of paper. You're going to title this paper "My Talents, Gifts, and Strengths." Make a list of all those things that you know so that you really list as many as possible.

- Quiet the negative chatter immediately, as soon as you begin to hear your brain tell you that "You're not good enough," "You're not enough," "You're not pretty enough," "You're not strong enough," "You're not smart enough." It's important for you to shut that down and immediately cancel those thoughts, even if you have to say "cancel" out loud! This is one of the tools that I have taught my children and family. When we state something negative about ourselves, statements like, "I can't do it," "I'm not smart enough," "I'm too fat," or "I'll never get through this," I tell them as well as I tell myself to say out loud "cancel, cancel." This allows you to mentally begin to cancel that negative thought pattern, and it allows for reprogramming your positive mindset.

- A lot of times when we have negative chatter, it comprises worries and concerns. It's a protective mechanism. This is because your brain always must look out for danger, whether it's a physical or mental danger. Your body is on the lookout all the time for you not to get your feelings hurt, not to feel like a failure, and not to feel pain. Believing that you can overcome anything in life with the right tools, like planning, strategies, and support—even learning new skills—can help you be confident and achieve your goals.

- Be gentle with yourself. You are just beginning your process of gaining confidence again. It's important to believe that we go through phases in life. For parts of your life, you may feel more confident than in others; just remember that it's a process, and there may be things that come up that you have to relearn over and over again as you build yourself up.

- Do not compare yourself to others. Comparing yourself to others is one of the quickest ways to lead you to negative thought patterns and feeling like you are not enough. It will cause you to backtrack on your confidence building as well as keep you stuck. Using social media has definitely taught us to compare and has kept us comparing ourselves to other people for many years now, and it can cause you to think that you are not enough or doing enough. I want you to remember that that is just someone's highlight reel. We don't see the crying in the corner that happens when all the shit hits the fan. So, just remember that as you scroll through social media and see everyone's amazing vacations and bodies and perfect relationships. Just know that that is their highlight reel and it's not the *real* story. Everyone is not what they "post" to be. Keep your eyes on your own paper, push forward, work only on what you can control, and do not compare your journey to someone else's.

- Surround yourself with positive people. It's important that you choose people to uplift you, not judge you, to help you continue the process of positive thinking about yourself. The people that you hang out with and talk to on a regular basis affect you more than you realize when it comes to making decisions about your life and even how you feel about yourself. I'm not just talking about friends; I'm talking about family as well. Sometimes the people who are closest to us don't always have our best interests in mind.

As you are building your self-confidence and self-esteem or just trying to maintain your self-confidence and self-esteem, remember to surround yourself with people who uplift you, who encourage you, who believe in you, and who don't try to dump their crap onto you. People will try to detour you from doing the things that they wish they had the confidence to do, so as you make changes, not everyone's going to be on board. There are going to be people who don't feel in alignment with you, and they don't agree with what you're doing because they don't believe that they can do it themselves as a result of their own negative thought patterns.

Don't let anyone stop you from creating the life that you really want. Find your tribe, find the people who are supportive and leave you feeling positive. One of the easiest ways to tell if someone is really in your corner or not is to see how you feel when you get off of the phone with them. See how you feel when you are not in their presence, see how you feel when you have left their presence. Do you feel inspired or drained? If you feel great, then you know that this is a friend who you want to be around more. If you feel drained and you feel not good about yourself after you have been with this person, this could be a toxic situation. There have been many friends that I've had who didn't necessarily say anything negative, or they may have said something that just left me feeling not great about myself. Many times, that friendship may be toxic and you either need to limit or eliminate the friend from being in your life.

One of the major things that needs to be considered (and we've talked about this in a previous chapter) is taking care of your body during this time as you are building your confidence. Don't take it lightly that your physical health impacts how you feel about yourself. How you look plays a part in your mental health and your self-confidence when you show up to business meetings, parenting, and relationships that are personal and professional. How you look does matter.

I know, I know, everyone says it's the inside that counts, and for the most part, I agree with that. However, I also know that how you feel and look on the outside sometimes shows how you feel on the inside. We always want our outside and inside to match up.

There is just something about exercise that automatically builds self-confidence. I don't know what magical things happen, but for some reason, confidence comes from putting your body under physical stress in the way of exercise and weight training. It allows you to see that not only can you mentally push through, but when you mentally push through, you can physically push through too. Once you begin to have more trust in yourself, even physically, the results are evident externally as well as internally. This is the point when you begin to trust yourself. Make sure to treat your body well while you are building or rebuilding your confidence. Don't ever forget that the physical aspect is just as important as the mental aspect, and you want to show up looking confident as well as feeling confident on the inside.

Show yourself some compassion. Treat yourself as you would treat a friend who you truly care about and love, or a family member who you truly care about and love. Talk to yourself as someone who is going through a hard time and wants to be uplifted. Show yourself kindness, compassion, and love, and give yourself some grace. You must be patient with yourself during this process, this process is a continuous journey. I want you to know that there's no destination when it comes to confidence. There will be times in our lives when we feel amazing and on top of the world, and there may be times in our lives when we feel that we cannot go on. What's most important is that we keep getting up.

THE ART OF SAYING NO

This was something that I learned when I was in Mexico, and I remember hearing it when I was at a conference. It wasn't your regular conference; it was a healing conference at an amazing resort called Rancho La Puerta. This resort is where people come to heal mentally and physically, it is not very far from San Diego. It is the most peaceful and beautiful space. There are many places to walk and gather your thoughts, as well as water fountains and mountains in the distance. While you are there, you eat nothing except plant-based food—no meat—and everything is grown in a garden nearby. It is marvelous! If you ever have the opportunity to go, it is worth it.

While I was there, I learned about healing some past traumas, and I remember our host and facilitator, Lisa Nichols, was guiding us on boundaries, and she said to us that no is a complete sentence. I had never heard this before. Basically, when you say no, you don't have to explain yourself. No is enough. I had never heard this before. How many times have you said no to someone but felt you needed to have a really good explanation of why the answer is no? Well, I release you from that today! No is complete, and you do not have to elaborate.

I think it's important to practice on a regular basis saying no to what you don't want. Say no to those things that you feel obligated to do. Unfortunately, many of us feel that we need to say yes to everything. I think it's easy for many of us to say yes because we are so good at multitasking and doing multiple things at one time. That doesn't necessarily mean that we need to be doing everything, especially tasks that are not going to be good for us or healthy for us.

Face your fears. Sometimes facing a new challenge allows you to tap into an inner strength that you did not have prior to overcoming that challenge. Facing challenges head-on allows you to strengthen your tenacity muscle, or muscles that you didn't know you had, period. What I would suggest is writing down things that you would like to accomplish that maybe you have been too nervous to even try to achieve. Now that you are beginning to get the tools to create the life that you want, it's time to look at the list of challenges. It's time to take a look at it and begin to face these challenges so that you can come out stronger on the other side.

My mentor, Lisa Nichols, says, "Even if your knees are shaking, you should do it anyway." Accomplishing challenges that are difficult or appear to be difficult continues to make you stronger and builds your confidence. It allows us to gather knowledge and tools for ourselves that we wouldn't ordinarily have unless we had pursued the challenge.

I recommend that you set challenges to conquer on a regular basis, and they don't always have to be a major dollar amount to obtain or a certain number of pounds to lose. It can be as simple as how much water you should drink daily. These things are small, but they can help us to begin to conquer and overcome larger challenges as time goes on.

The times when I have a big challenge in front of me, I am so terrified, especially if it's a speaking engagement somewhere. I get nervous and I may not feel that I'm able to accomplish it; however, once I'm done, I feel so relieved and empowered! That's the kind of power that you can't get from anywhere else; you can only get it from yourself by overcoming that challenge. In July of 2020, I pitched my business to a group of people, quite frankly unseen, because this was in the middle of the COVID-19 pandemic and we couldn't see each other, we had to be on Zoom, and I was the only African American woman that was scheduled to present. I felt a lot of pressure going up against five to six other males who seemed like they had it way more together than me, and I pulled together all of the information I needed to pitch. I'd never ever pitched my business before, and after working so hard and rehearsing my pitch, I won that pitch and I beat everyone else, and won a cash prize of $3,000!

This was my first time pitching ever! But one of the reasons I won was because of the confidence I showed up with from research, studying, and rehearsing. Confidence matters! I pitched for the first time and won first place! After it was over, I felt so empowered and even more confident about my business abilities. I felt so empowered, I was ready to pitch my business again. This was one of the things that I was always terrified to do. I thought there was no way that I could ever pitch my business, and after going through that experience, I know I have what it takes to go into any room and pitch my business. But that could have only come from me standing up to my fear of just not knowing what to do and not knowing how to do it. Now I have something that no one can ever take away, which is that experience and all that I learned from it.

Confidence builds up over time and experiences. There may be times in your life when you feel super confident, everything is going as it should, and you feel like you're super knowledgeable. Then there might be other areas of your life when you may not feel so confident, such as how you look, how you speak, how you present, how you date, or even your career. If there's an area of your life that you feel you would like to feel stronger in, use some of the tips above to help strengthen your confidence, and know that it's always a journey.

As your life changes, your confidence changes due to the challenges of life, a death in the family, becoming ill, getting married, or having a baby. The circumstances that surround your life will change, as you go along your journey, realize that there may be moments when you have to strengthen certain areas of your life. Everyone has their own journey; do not compare your journey to anyone else's.

CONFIDENCE VS. SELF-ESTEEM

I referenced before that we hear so many times about faking it till you make it. Is there a difference between confidence and self-esteem? What I'm really talking about in this book is building your self-esteem so that you can have more confidence. It's not about working from the outside in, it's about working from the inside out. The better your self-esteem, the more confidence will exude from you. Confidence won't be something that you have to focus on or concentrate on, you will just be confident. I want to encourage you as you read this book to build up your confidence so you can have more power to level up in all areas of your life. Know that confidence has to start with how you feel about yourself first and that it's always going to start with your self-esteem.

Self-esteem is an individual's observation and evaluation of their own self-worth. Self-esteem encompasses so many different things, from your relationships and emotional health to your overall well-being, your perspective on life, and how you make your decisions. Self-esteem is like an internal compass. I would classify myself as one of the good girlfriends that everyone calls to talk to about their relationship problems. It has been like this for me ever since I was in high school. I have been the person that people come to whenever they have issues with their relationships. At a very young age, friends would come to me with advice. After listening to many different stories, I realized that my friends were making decisions based on how they felt about themselves, not strictly based on the facts. No matter how I felt about them—even if I thought they were amazing, powerful, strong, and influential—if that person didn't feel the way, then they made decisions from their compass point—from a navigational system that was altered and flawed.

As a mom, it was important to me to make sure that I raised my children to have a healthy internal navigation or internal compass above all else. Self-esteem is how you can truly gauge where and how you are making the decisions in your life. I always tell everyone that where you are today is based on all of the decisions that you made up to this point, good, bad, and ugly. You have gotten yourself to the point where you are today. You definitely cannot control what other people have done to you, but you can definitely control what you have done with the information and the circumstances that you have been dealt. I encourage you, if you really want true self-confidence and the confidence that exudes in every aspect of your life, work on your self-esteem, because if you don't and a situation comes along that disrupts your lifestyle or your life—such as life milestones—your entire life can come tumbling down without a solid foundation.

How do you know if you have low self-esteem? You will know by the areas of your life and the decisions you have made. Like I've said in previous chapters, you may feel really strong and confident in one area of your life, such as your career or job, but you might feel less confident about sharing your emotions. You can feel confident in different areas of your life.

Self-esteem is that internal compass that guides every single decision you make, so if you have low self-esteem, there are some things you may find yourself doing in your life that you wish you could change.

As I wrote this book, I learned something about self-esteem that was shocking, even to me. I think most of us think that people with low self-esteem walk around with their heads hanging low, looking depressed. You'd be very surprised what some of the major signs of low self-esteem look like.

What does poor self-esteem really look like? Low self-esteem can be doubting yourself and being unsure of your decisions. It's also not being able to express your wants and needs at work and in your personal relationships. You might not have the courage to actually try new things because you are so afraid that you might fail. People with low self-esteem internally feel unworthy or that they're not deserving of the things that they really want in life. Some of this may resonate with you as it did with me. I have felt like this on many different occasions.

You definitely want to work on your self-esteem. Having too much self-esteem can be dangerous also because you can be someone who feels that they are entitled regardless of whether or not they have the abilities or skills. Many people struggle with relationships and don't really care to improve themselves. They think that there's nothing really wrong with them or that there's no room for improvement, and that's a very dangerous space to be.

You will always want to be "a student of life" and be willing to learn and grow. Acting more arrogant is not what we are aiming for, because we know that no one is good at everything all the time in their life. It will be important for you to get to know yourself so that you are aware of your strengths and weaknesses. Self-esteem will play a big part in whether you're able to achieve your goals or not able to achieve your goals. It's always an inside job first, and healthy self-esteem comes before true confidence.

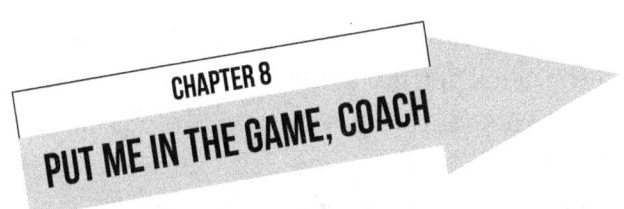

CHAPTER 8
PUT ME IN THE GAME, COACH

"The delicate balance of mentoring someone is not creating them in your own image, but giving them the opportunity to create themselves."
—Steven Spielberg

Coaching helps you get to your goals quicker, faster, sooner. Have you ever had a goal that you wanted to achieve, but you felt that something was in your way or that you were just climbing toward this goal going uphill? Receiving coaching or being mentored allows you to achieve goals that you otherwise could not achieve by yourself. There was a point in my life when I had first started my practice and I felt I did not know what I was doing. I started my practice in a cute little place in Sandston, Virginia, which is not far from Richmond. I pretty much opened this office based on the thought that the building looked very appealing and it was on a main road. It was not the greatest business decision, but these are the decisions that you make when you have no guidance. You base things off of how a building looks or if it's close to your house or not, when it's really all about location, location, location. I was blessed enough to actually open my practice in this location on the main strip, but I didn't know anything else about starting a business.

I didn't know how to market; all I knew was to contact the people that I had seen before, and hopefully on the first day that I opened, someone might be there on the books. If I had a coach at that time, I would have made a lot of different decisions. I would have started marketing earlier than a couple of weeks before or a month before. I would have purchased certain equipment to build out my office and known how long it was going to take me to build up my clientele. I also would have known how to continue to market even after I opened the doors to practice. I didn't know any of these things; I was strictly going on that I knew how to be a great chiropractor.

Having a coach would have helped me to not have to feel like I was struggling for so many years in practice, and I would have been able to take my practice to another level instead of struggling year after year. Sometimes after you've been in business for a while with no help, it feels like it's not for you; it feels like you can't achieve the goals that you really want to achieve. But if you have a mentor who's been in your shoes, someone who is ten steps ahead of you and can help you achieve your goals, it's so much faster. The mistakes I made I would not have made.

While I was in practice, I would have known to put a sign out ahead of time to market to potential patients and let them know that I was opening up. I would have avoided a lot of mistakes that most business owners make. Most business owners think that they know everything because they went to school. As an employee, you think you know everything about how to excel or succeed and that you can do it so much better than your boss. It is once you own a business of your own that you see the challenges that stand before you, and if you have no mentor, you have no guidance. There are so many different things you don't know that you can learn from someone who has gone and walked in the same footsteps.

What a mentor or coach can do is help you quantum-leap and skip so many of those steps that I mentioned above where I failed. But you don't know what you don't know. Mentors can help you to save money and heartache, save you from the emotional anguish of thinking you are just dumb, stupid, and never going to succeed. At the time, I didn't know that a coach was what I needed. I thought I had all the information I needed to succeed in practice. No one told me I might need an actual coach until I spoke with a doctor who is super successful in Philadelphia. She is an African American woman like me and has been very successful in the chiropractic game. Her name is Dr. Corrine Morgan. This woman is a chiropractic icon in my eyes. They even have her face on the wall of Palmer College of Chiropractic in Davenport, Iowa, as a trailblazer for women. I reached out to her when I was working as an independent chiropractor looking for some advice, and that is when she led me to my first coach, Dr. Chandler George. Once hired, he helped me navigate many challenges of business and taught me so many things that I would have never learned on my own.

I highly recommend and believe in great coaching or great mentorship, whether you want to be one for yourself or someone else. I recommend that you get multiple coaches. Different coaches specialize in different topics. There is no one-size-fits-all approach to coaching, and one coach may not be able to supply all of your needs. If you want to get to certain places in your life, whether it's in a relationship, business, your personal life, or your health, you need coaching.

Sometimes, people do not need a coach. They actually need to seek outside mental health support to proceed. Coaching is not therapy. It is important to seek out mental health support prior to or while you are receiving coaching. I had the pleasure of coaching someone who was a very prominent figure in her community, and she was suffering from some mental health challenges at the time I took her on as a coaching client. I took her on as a client to help her, but ultimately this person really needed more mental health care and less coaching. So, I referred her back to her mental health provider. Your coach is not your therapist. You may need to seek out mental health support prior to coaching, depending on where you are in your life. Don't mistake mental health care for coaching or vice versa. When you approach coaching, you need to be in a really good mental space. You need to be in a space where you are open to learning new things, and you have to be coachable.

So how do you know if you are ready to be coached? How do you know if coaching is right for you? Coaching is for someone who is ready to go to the next level, ready to be the best version of themselves. Coaching is also for someone who wants to be guided, who does not feel that they have all the answers to their life. Coaching is for someone who is ready to be honest with themselves and what they are weak in or what they want to get stronger in. It will not serve you to finally commit to going to a coach or a therapist and not be honest with yourself or your coach about where you are. You have to be willing to be honest with your coach and you also have to be willing to trust them. Trust that they are going to give you the best answer possible when it comes to the challenges in your life or business, or whatever area that they're coaching you in.

Hiring a coach who is right for you is important. You want to pick a coach who is supportive of your dreams and not competing with you or discouraging you. If you just want to build more confidence in yourself, your coach is going to cheer you on to the next level and hold you accountable—something that we all need in our lives.

How do you find the right coach for you? What I encourage people to do when they are ready to actually find a coach is to understand that one coach can't do everything, so you may have to hire more support. I have a multitude of coaches: a productivity coach, a spiritual coach, a business coach, and a speaker coach. I have had many different types of coaches that have helped me strengthen different areas of my life.

When you decide to pick your coach, I suggest you start on social media. Find people that you like to watch and just watch them for a while. This is your time to research what these coaches may have to offer. Sometimes they have offers that are free, which gives you an opportunity to try their services. Use social media to dive into their content on all social media platforms. Look at their YouTube, look at their Facebook and Instagram.

When you get hooked on their page, turn on the notifications so that when they are posting, you don't miss it. Often these coaches will have special offerings that you can catch on sale. This gives you the opportunity to purchase from them without breaking the bank.

Before investing in one of the high-ticket items, I always suggest looking at what they have for free. Lots of times, people give bits and pieces of information for free online and then you can work up to paying for one of their programs. There is so much free information out there online that you can use. Coaches are constantly giving away programs and services at a low cost for you to get to know them better. I suggest that if you do not have a budget for coaching, start with the free items that they have on their page. Watch their videos and scroll their page so you can get to know them really well before you invest.

Research to see if you like their energy. Do you feel like you want to be in their vortex? One of the best signs to decide if that person is the right coach for you is if they are resonating with you just from their presence on social media. Any coaching is an investment. It is something that you will see a return on. Sometimes the return is not immediate. You have to be clear on what you want from your coach.

When I was searching for a coach to help me transition from practicing to doing more speaking, I sought out one coach in particular. Her name is Lisa Nichols, and I went to her for advice. I wanted her to tell me what to do and how to do it. That is not the job of a coach. Many times, she would ask me questions for clarity. In the beginning, I did not have an answer because I wasn't clear about my dreams. Until I could get clear and ask the right questions, I stayed stuck. When you decide that you are ready to be a coaching client, be prepared to do some soul searching for what you really want to get out of life, as well as what you want to get from your coach. Your coach will not tell you what your purpose is; they will want you to come prepared and ready with that information. Unless you hire a coach who can dig deep to get it out of you. There is literally a coach for anything and everything under the sun.

Coaches are going to help you increase your revenue, create a strategy, and get clearer on how to slay your goals quicker, faster, sooner. Having a coach helps to give you peace of mind. Coaches can help build your confidence and push you forward in your business and knock your goals out of the park. When your budget permits, move forward past the free content to a paid program. As you learn more tools and use them to make more money, then you can move to the larger investments.

If you find a coach who you really like on social media, move forward by either reaching out to them, getting on a discovery call, or trying to find some of those fifteen-minute calls that are free where they can tell you what they offer. In the end, they may try to get you to sign up for a program, but at least you can hear their voice and hear if you like their energy.

I believe that you will find the right coach for you, and it'll be such a connection and flow that you will know that they are the right coach for you and that they fit into your budget. Please don't feel anxious or discouraged if you can't find the right coach for you. You might not be ready to fly to Florida for the Tony Robbins experience; that's okay, there are a lot of other amazing coaches. There are coaches out there who may not be well-known but still have great information and so much to offer. Find a coach within your budget and go for it.

Coaching programs are out there to help you make more money and be happier. Just remember that there are many different coaches out there who will suit you, and I've even had different coaches teach me the similar concepts, so just be open that there are many ways to learn about a topic. You may hear information from one coach and then go to another coach and hear it in a different way. It depends on where you are in your life that allows you to be open to receiving information. I just encourage everyone to be open to different coaching styles.

Be willing to receive support from coaches who suit you better for different areas of your life. Just don't expect one coach to be all of everything. Coaches have different gifts and talents in certain areas, so make sure you're finding the right coach who is good for you in the area that you want to excel in and go to the next level.

Be prepared to be coached. A great coach wants you to succeed. You are not paying them to tell you that you have done everything perfectly and correctly. If that is what you are looking for, coaching is not a place for you. Coaching is not about only hearing what you want to hear about yourself. You must be open to feedback and trying things in a different way. You will not hear exactly what you want to hear. Be ready for this when you decide to be coached or mentored.

Be coachable. This is what always plays in my head when I have a long talk with my own coaches. I had a coach one time tell me quite frankly many things about my business that I did not like. Honestly, sometimes I would get off the phone and be so upset with him. He told me, "It's not my job to tell you what you want to hear, it's my job to help you grow and learn and work on areas that will help you grow."

I don't think that when you find a coach you should feel completely miserable after a session. Instead, you should realize that they're not there to tell you everything that you want to hear and that you are amazing. You have hired them to stretch you so that you are willing to push forward and leap past your limits. They should hold you accountable for the actions you intend to take. You may feel uncomfortable; that's okay, as long as you are growing and learning in the area you hired them to help you. I have had to actually fire a coach after I felt that they had crossed the line. You may have to do that as well.

You have to find a coach who is willing to be gentle with you and be honest with you. You want your coach to be willing to tell you the truth but also be willing to be gentle enough to know that you need encouragement to be pushed forward. Your coach should be your biggest cheerleader and praise your success. Be leery of the coaches who get insecure or jealous about your big dreams. No coach is perfect, but they should want to see you succeed and cheer you all the way to the top. That is why, when you choose a coach, make sure that they are ten to twenty steps ahead of you so that there is no competition while they coach you.

In conclusion, one of the reasons that coaching is so important is if you desire to coach others, it's important to show up as the best version of yourself. By investing in yourself, you will be in the position to help so many other people, whether you are in business for yourself or for your family. You can never go wrong with investing in yourself. If you don't invest in yourself, don't expect others to do so. We all need help reaching our goals; no one does it alone.

Building yourself back up again has to do with internal power. There was a young lady one time who came to me and asked me for business coaching. She ran a daycare and was really doing amazing things in the community. Her business helped students find daycare and after-school care for kids whose parents were working. I thought this was such a great and noble thing and she was really helping the community. One of the things that she was struggling with was collecting the payment. She was allowing people to pay once a week and sometimes two weeks later. People were getting in the rear with their payments, and it was just devastating to her business. This was really challenging. I made some recommendations and explained to her that by allowing people to pay late, she was demonstrating a lack of boundaries. As a business owner, she thought she was doing them a favor by allowing them not to pay on time. I was able to coach her through this rough patch in her business to get her back on track to getting money and keeping money in her pockets. While coaching her, I told her that the biggest thing that she could do for her community was to stay in business. The meaning behind one of my real-life coaching stories is that the best thing you can do for your community and your family is to be a healthy, happy person. But you must show up for yourself first. I know my coaching client was happy we were able to increase her revenue, which allowed her to stay in business, set boundaries, and build her confidence around accepting payments.

Coaching will help you go further faster. Helping people in this area is what I do best. If this is something that you need help with or want some advice with, please go to my website to schedule a strategy call. I help professionals and entrepreneurs get clarity, create a vision, gain confidence, and take the big leaps to live their greatest life. I do this through my coaching, courses, and online and in-person experiences. I support go-getter women to get clear, know their value, create a plan, and create the life they deserve. Many men and women go further and faster toward their dreams when they invest in a coach. If you would like to schedule a call to see if I can help you, please visit my website www.doctorneema.com to schedule a strategy session today.

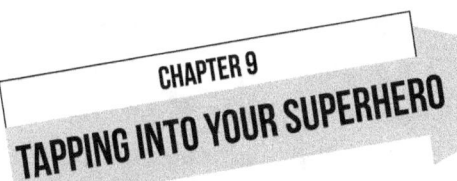

CHAPTER 9
TAPPING INTO YOUR SUPERHERO

*"Heroes are made by the path they choose,
not the powers they are graced with."*

—Iron Man

Tap into your superhero. Tapping into your superhero is when you bring everything together that we have talked about in the previous chapters. I want you to know that you have the power within you to create the life that you truly want. By following some of the ideas, tips, and tools in this book, you can begin to truly create the life that you want. It's not about a destination; it will always be about the journey. There is no final destination when it comes to your growth or your progress. Becoming your highest self and your best version of yourself is a marathon, not a sprint.

As you reflect on parts of this book that you have read, you may be using what you have read as a measurement of how you have been doing in life. It is true that whatever you have accomplished up until this point is a sum of your decisions. The decisions you have made were based on the information that you had at that time in your life. Some of the things that you have learned in your past from your past experiences have been so deeply ingrained in you that they are very difficult to undo. It takes time to unlearn all that we have learned from our childhoods, our parents, bad experiences, bad relationships, and even adult experiences in our lives. Please give yourself grace as you begin to learn to do life in a new way that serves you better.

It takes a lot of time to practice an intention, to begin to change these old habits that are so deeply ingrained in your life. Quite frankly, sometimes you're just tired and you don't feel like doing the work, but I promise you, if you decide to do the work, it will pay off in your relationships, businesses, and your overall success. But my friends, this is the long haul, and taking the time out to be more conscious of how you walk this life journey will really benefit you as you have more challenging life experiences. When you start to be hard on yourself, I want you to think of a baby. When a baby is beginning to walk, they stumble and fall because their muscles are not strong enough to walk yet. They are still learning and growing. We are not harsh on them and do not yell at them; we are gentle and encouraging. Remember to be kind to yourself in the same way. Learning the things that we have talked about here in this book is also like learning to walk in some cases. You may fall down, you may make mistakes, but what does a parent or caretaker do when they see a child trying to walk for the first time? We cheer them on. It is so exciting; it's amazing, they're learning something new! I want you to think of yourself as that new child learning to walk. If these things are just very new to you and it's like moving a muscle that you have not strengthened yet, I want you to cheer yourself on. I want you to clap, yell, jump up, give yourself a big hug and a kiss, and recognize that you will get better at this as time goes on.

Tapping into your superhero strength is knowing that you have the power within. We can't always see it, but the power is still there. You know, one of the great things about Superman is that he is Clark Kent during the daytime, and he is Superman at night. Spiderman is, a young kid during the daytime, and in some movies, he's a student during the day or a lab technician during the day and he is saving the world at night. Regardless of either superhero or situation, their power is still there within them even if other people can't see it.

You may feel that you or other people can't see your power, and sometimes you know that it's there. However, others are not recognizing it and that's okay, because it's really not about them recognizing your power; it's about you recognizing your power and knowing when to use it and how to use it properly to serve other people.

Here is an exercise I want you to try. I want you to imagine what the best version of yourself looks like in your mind—and realize that over time, as you have other experiences, that version of you will change. For now, write down what you think the best version of *you* looks like. What type of clothes do you wear now? What do you look like? How do you speak? What do you do when you're sad? What do you do when you're happy? What do you do for fun? What type of food do you eat? What type of places do you go to?

Ask yourself some of these questions to get down to the core of who you are trying to become as you begin to pull yourself out of the challenging times in your life. Creating confidence and getting back to who you are may take a little bit of time. Ultimately, your superhero and your superhero powers can only be defined by you. Don't get nervous if you see your superpower in another superhero, it's okay if many of us are trying to save the world. It's going to take all of us to make positive encounters with so many different people in the world, and your voice and your power matter just as much as the next superhero.

One of the things that I love about every superhero movie is that there's always this moment where the superhero doesn't know that they have the power. They take us through this in almost every movie where in the beginning they are unaware of the power they hold inside. As challenges go on throughout the movie, they realize their power, or someone has to tell them to believe in themselves.

Well, we are here. We are at that part of the book where I am telling you to believe in yourself, that you do have the power within you, and that you do have what it takes to achieve and create the life that you truly want. Guess what? Everyone does not want the same thing, so don't get into the pattern of jealousy or thinking that somebody can take something from you. We all want different things, therefore, there's enough to go around for everyone. Taking your power back and using your power in the correct way will not only change your life, but it can change the lives of the people around you. I want to encourage you to take the time out for yourself, to encourage yourself, nourish yourself, and give yourself the grace that you need as you build your confidence. By using some of the tools in this book, you will start to see a difference in what you are capable of doing and what you are attracting in your life.

Our world needs you. You're not too late, you're not too early, you're not too old, and you're not too young to live your biggest, wildest dreams. You matter. Your life matters. And we need you to show up. Because the best thing you can do for the world and for your life is to be the happiest, healthiest version of yourself.

Ultimately, remember that you have the power within. Most of what you need is inside of yourself. There may be times when you need to reach out to other health professionals, coaches, or mentors to help you get over this challenge, and I want to encourage you to do that. Don't be afraid to ask for the help you need so that you can create the life you truly desire. It's not a sign that you are incompetent or don't have what it takes to succeed. Life is a journey, and it is a marathon, not a race. Your journey will be up and down, and just like the seasons that we have in nature, you have seasons of life. Sometimes it's the season to plant, sometimes it's the season to harvest, sometimes it's the season of rest, and sometimes it's the season of play.

The season you're in will determine what you need to support yourself in mind, body, and spirit. Please don't compare yourself to others when you go on social media and see everyone's highlight reels. That's exactly what it is—it is a highlight reel of their life; it is not a true reality. Because who wants to post when they're failing endlessly or about being heartbroken and having their feelings hurt? No one is going to post that, but don't think it's not happening in everyone's lives, because we're all human. This is one of my favorite sayings that I have said earlier in the book, and it means don't compare yourself to others. Your journey is your journey, and it will be different because you are different.

If you are in a time of challenge in your life or you are in a time of building your self-confidence back up, give yourself some grace. Speak to yourself as you would speak to a good friend whom you really love and care about. Quiet the negative chatter that says you're not good enough, you're not pretty enough, you're not strong enough, and you're just not enough. You are enough if you are reading this—that means that you're still alive, you're still breathing, and you have a functional brain that can process complicated information and that means there is always and will always be hope for you. Hold on to that hope, never let it go, and no matter what, never ever give up on yourself.

CHAPTER 10
NOW GO AND BE GREAT

"Nothing liberates our greatness like the desire to help, the desire to serve."
—Marianne Williamson

If you have gotten this far in the book, let me just say congratulations! You made it! I dropped a lot of things to add to your already-busy schedule in this book. If you're like me, you read a book and forget some of the ideas in it. I want to encourage you to take out your pen and paper and go back through this book multiple times. I wrote this book to feel more like a manual that you can use and come back to. Continue to work on the things in this book every day in your life. It is truly a process to reprogram your mind from what it has been thinking and doing for years. Deciding to make changes in your life is not easy. The naysayers and the negativity will always be background noise. Don't worry, that's normal. We all have negative background noise. The goal is to find ways to block it out and do what you were created to do, follow your purpose, and bring your passion with you. There are many things to try in this book, and as we finish our time here, I want to encourage you to choose just one thing that you can implement into your daily life. Change is very difficult for all of us. Here is a suggestion—try to implement one new thing every quarter. It takes the mind and body sixty-six days to learn a new habit, so give yourself time to develop a new habit.

When pilots fly a plane, they have to set the latitude and longitude of where they are going. The exact degree allows them to get to their destination. Changing one degree will have the plane end up at an entirely different location, about one mile for every degree that was mis programmed. One mile away from your destination is not very extreme, but if you were walking, would you want to be one mile from your destination?

This is an example of how trying these tools or tips can actually change the direction of your life for the better. The overall undertone of this book is that simple, consistent small steps over time are all it takes. Slow and steady will always win the race toward confidence mastery. Be gentle with yourself along the way as you learn new ways to navigate this amazing journey we call life.

I want to encourage you to never stop learning and growing. Unfortunately, age has nothing to do with maturity and growth. And as the world around you forever changes, you must change with it if you want personal growth and to become the best version of yourself. I imagine that if you are reading this book, you want to learn and grow to be a better person. Not everyone will understand the importance of doing what I have stated in this book. Please understand there will be many times you travel this personal mastery journey alone. Do it anyway. The rewards are massive and will affect the generations that come after you.

Do it anyway. The journey will be long, but it will be worth it. Keep the faith and never give up on yourself or your dreams. It always seems impossible until it's done. Never stop dreaming.

Never give up.

"You must be the change you wish to see in the world."
—Mahatma Gandhi

ABOUT THE AUTHOR

Dr. Neema Tillery Moore is passionate about helping woman professionals and entrepreneurs gain the clarity, and confidence they need to achieve their goals.

Dr. Moore earned her bachelor of science in biology from Elizabeth City State University and her doctor of chiropractic from Palmer College of Chiropractic. In addition to owning her own business, Wellness Within, Dr. Moore is a chiropractor and confidence coach who specializes in helping women optimize their health, maximize their gifts, and help them to take the big leap to create the life of their dreams.

Dr. Moore currently resides in Northern Virginia with her husband. She is a wife to another entrepreneur and the mother of twins. She loves being a mom, being in nature, traveling the world, and reading personal development books.

To connect, email her at
Drneema@wellnesswithinva.com

CREATING DISTINCTIVE BOOKS WITH INTENTIONAL RESULTS

We're a collaborative group of creative masterminds with a mission to produce high-quality books to position you for monumental success in the marketplace.

Our professional team of writers, editors, designers, and marketing strategists work closely together to ensure that every detail of your book is a clear representation of the message in your writing.

Want to know more?
Write to us at info@publishyourgift.com
or call (888) 949-6228

Discover great books, exclusive offers, and more at
www.PublishYourGift.com

Connect with us on social media

@publishyourgift

www.ingramcontent.com/pod-product-compliance
Lightning Source LLC
Chambersburg PA
CBHW052207090526
44583CB00016BA/1764